VISUALIZE YOURSELF

DESIGNING THE OUTCOME OF YOUR LIFE, ONE ISSUE AT A TIME

Aileen Nealie, LMFT, DCEP

Cover illustration by Kelly Barrow

authorHOUSE®

AuthorHouse™ LLC
1663 Liberty Drive
Bloomington, IN 47403
www.authorhouse.com
Phone: 1-800-839-8640

Published by AuthorHouse   08/08/2013

ISBN: 978-1-4918-0346-2 (sc)
ISBN: 978-1-4918-0345-5 (e)

Library of Congress Control Number: 2013913759

Any people depicted in stock imagery provided by Dreamstime are models, and such images are being used for illustrative purposes only. Certain stock imagery © Dreamstime.

This book is printed on acid-free paper.

CONTENTS

Part III: Transcending the Vision

To my son, Sebastian Sunny, whose existence I visualized for over five years, and who granted me the manifestation of a masterpiece by joining me in this lifetime.

INTRODUCTION

Ever since I can remember, I have been utilizing the beauty of daydreaming—that is *visualization*—to design the outcome of my life. As I see it, visualization is just like daydreaming. When you give purpose to your daydreaming experiences, you are that much closer to fulfilling your dreams. Therefore, visualization is a natural process. This process can also be fun and extremely powerful. How many times have we heard others say, "It all starts with a dream"? All it takes is focus, intention, and creativity, which everyone possesses. Yet not everyone taps into these natural skills as often or as thoroughly as they could in order to benefit from them.

Now, before you begin doubting yourself, I want to give you a formula that you can cater to your personal style. Let us go back to the word *creativity*. Even before we begin daydreaming, we engage in imaginary play. Little girls begin with dolls and play out elaborate stories that they come up with. Some of this comes from what they watch and hear from others, but some comes from their imaginations. We may also refer to this as their fantasy world. Boys do the same with action heroes.

Go back to your early childhood, and think of a theme that you liked to incorporate in play. This was my experience: my dolls were two sisters, who were always going into the woods to find animals. Along their path they would give a voice to everything alive. The trees talked, the rocks talked, the birds were fairies, and the owls were wizards that gave the dolls magical powers to change everything they touched into candy.

It is your turn now. Visually transport yourself to an age when your imagination was completely free from limitations and doubts. Try to remember a recurring theme for daydreaming or playing. Allow your imagination to go with it. Immerse yourself into whatever it is you fantasized about. Notice how your body feels. Relax. If doubts or fears are coming up, work through some of the visualizations in this book, which are purposed to help you to release them. If you feel the easiness, then pick an area of your life or something about yourself that you would like to change. Start creating a story—a new story that is limitless and that makes it all just right. Stick to your story and elaborate on it every day. Give it color; give it flavor; give it love. Live this story every day until you *become* the story—until your reality is this new story. Yes, you can!

If you have doubts, think about our childhood imaginary friends. These friends seem to be erased from our memory once we reach adulthood. How terribly sad! Can it be possible that we *disallow* ourselves to imagine? Is there a switch within us that gets turned off once we join "the real world"? Wait! *Which is the real world?*

Visualization, creativity, imagination, daydreaming, magic—I will use these terms interchangeably when referring to the ability to visualize yourself. I visualize most easily with my eyes closed. And yes, as a matter of fact, I wrote this book with my eyes closed. I recorded myself and then transcribed it. I guess I can say I created this book by daydreaming.

As a psychotherapist, I use visualization quite often with my patients, individually or in groups. I get to see the magic taking place within them as they travel with their eyes closed. I hear and watch their emotions, their processing, their healing, their *aha* moments, their belief in themselves, their belief in what they want, and their need to become whole. It's all happening at once. Yes, it is real. Then, as time goes on and we have further visits, I get to witness the magic become a reality. These individuals begin to integrate their spirits, their bodies, and their minds to be in harmony with the new reality they have created for themselves. In turn, my daydreaming also becomes a reality, as I am able to enjoy the rewards of helping others and watching them get what they wished for.

Who says life has to be difficult? Well, adults do. Who has proven that life flows and is easy? Well, children have. How do you want to lead your life? Well, you decide. With this book I am attempting to help you remember the easy way. I hope you choose this route. Dare to come out of your shell and play in the magical kingdom to create YOUR real world.

PART I

Focusing the Lens of Your Visualization

1. VISUALIZATION 101

It is very common to confuse visualization with meditation. Visualization is the art of designing an outcome visually, in order to manifest it. Visualization can be accomplished anytime, anywhere. For instance, you can be daydreaming while you ride the subway to work, giving shape and color to a project. You can do the same while putting together a vision board, as you collect pictures and imagine how your life will turn out. However, the practice of centering and creating a soothing place can help you maximize your visualization experience. In this respect, it is similar to meditation; as is the goal to silence the thoughts and allow the higher self to provide you with insight, clarity, answers, and peace. Since our thoughts create doubts, they get in the way of the purity of our visions. Therefore, achieving a meditative state is highly recommended until you master your ability to focus.

For example, the heaven and earth balancing visual, which you will find in Part II, Section 8, is the one visual that I follow as one patient enters and the other exits my office. It is completed within a blink of an eye. I can do this because I practice it so very often. However, when I teach it to others, I ask them to close their eyes and use their breath to center, so they are able to understand their internal responses and see through their third eye (the point right between the eyebrows where wisdom and intellect energetically reside). Therefore, I highly recommend that you follow the steps outlined in Part I, Section 1 and use the breathing visual found in Part I, Section 2 to help you center even more prior to each visualization piece in this book.

At times you may go very deep into your subconscious. When this happens, your physical body may not be fully present. This is the reason why some people may feel cold, hot, or tingly during their visualization work. One person may experience a different sensation each time he or she goes through a visualization script.

Visualization is not hypnosis. However, when you allow your thoughts to fully silence, your brainwaves become much slower. The three most common brainwave frequencies reached while in meditation are alpha, delta, and theta. *Finerminds.com* describes entering each of the three stages. Reaching alpha is described as follows: "Alpha brainwaves are present in deep relaxation and usually when the eyes are closed, when you're slipping into a lovely daydream or during light meditation. It is an optimal time to program the mind for success, and it also heightens your imagination, visualization, memory, learning, and concentration." The site also describes going into delta: "This frequency is the slowest of the frequencies and is experienced in deep, dreamless sleep and in very deep, transcendental meditation where awareness is fully detached. It is the realm of your unconscious mind and the gateway to the universal mind and the collective unconscious, where information received is otherwise unavailable at the conscious level." And finally, theta is addressed: "It is said that a sense of deep spiritual connection and unity with the universe can be experienced at theta. Your mind's most deep-seated programs are at theta, and it is where you experience vivid visualizations, great inspiration, profound creativity, and exceptional insight. Unlike your other brainwaves, the elusive voice of theta is a silent voice."

Every new experience has a beginning stage. Pace yourself and allow yourself to evolve with visualization. Don't try to compare yourself to other visualizers. The experiences are unique, just as each person's life is completely unique from another's. And just as we cannot live anyone else's life, nor can they live ours. It takes time and practice, yet with the right intentions, you will soon be successfully designing the outcome of your life, one issue at a time.

2. Preparing For Visualization

Follow these instructions prior to beginning any visualization. Visualization is most effective when you create a peaceful setting for yourself. This may be different from person to person. However, following are some suggestions you can utilize as a starting point:

- Find a quiet place, either inside or outside in nature (never while driving!).
- Light a candle (as many as you would like).
- Burn incense or spray the space you are in with aromatherapy essences.
- Utilize soft, soothing, and relaxing music.
- Either sit or lie down (although lying down may make you sleepy).
- Close your eyes. I realize that may not be possible if you are reading the script. However, you may have a friend or relative

read it for you, or you may choose to record the script with your voice and play it back as a guide. You may even choose to memorize it and silently recall it while in a meditative state.

- Have drinking water always within reach.

- Release all expectations.

- Be in the *now*.

- You may choose to use the breathing visualization in Part I, Section 2 to help you center.

Once your setting is to your liking, begin to focus on your breath. Inhale through your nose and exhale through your mouth. Allow your breath to take its natural course until it becomes easier to take deeper breaths. The goal is to be able to breathe deeply until you fill up your lungs with new oxygen, and slowly expell just as when deflating a balloon. Next, as you become centered, try to release all expectations. If you are spiritually inclined, invoke assistance from the ascended masters, angels, your higher self, God, the universe, the sun, nature, universal healing energy, etc. Your spiritual believes can only enhance the purity of your experiences. However, if you are not spiritual, you can still achieve results. It is all about setting an intention within your heart. Now you are ready to begin your journey.

Additional Tips

It is a given that most individuals are very busy these days. All of us have responsibilities and to-do lists.

Therefore, it is not uncommon to have your thoughts interfere with your process. When this occurs, simply go back to your breath. There may be times when you are able to disconnect from your thoughts better than at other times. This is the reason why it is so important to release any expectations. You will attain what you are ready to attain from that particular visualization experience. Even when you go over the same visualization CD or script, you can be certain that there will always be a different experience in store for you. Just go with it and allow it to unfold for you. In other words, do not force it to happen.

The reason I suggest that you have water within reach is because, like a physical workout, visualization can be draining, especially when you are releasing and restoring your energy field. Therefore hydration is imperative.

Centering

In case you do not know this from meditation, the easiest way to center yourself and clear the interference of your thoughts is by focusing on your breath. With each inhalation and exhalation you are bringing in new oxygen and recycling the old. The traditional "inhale through your nose and exhale through your mouth" applies in every instance. Now, since my job is to help you make this process a fun one, I will share with you a sequence of breathing like no other. Remember, although you will always use your inhalations and exhalations with the following visuals, these breaths will start and will end at different parts of your body. So get ready for centering with your breath.

The Journey of Your Breath

>First, pay attention to your breathing pattern
>and then slowly begin to inhale through your

nose, taking in enough air to fill your lungs. Then exhale by releasing all that air through your mouth. Now, try that same breathing again, except this time begin inhaling through your tail bone, bringing all the air through your spine, the back of your neck, and head, and then exhaling right between your eyes (your third eye). Next, inhale through your navel, allowing the breath to travel through your legs, and exhale through the bottom of your feet. Then, inhale through your throat, let the air travel through your arms, and exhale through your fingertips. Once again, inhale through your navel, letting the breath continue through your chest and throat, and exhale above your head.

Continue inhaling and filling up the entire interior of your physical body, and as you exhale, envision the breath expelling through every pore. Watch now, as your breath has externalized, and invite it to dance around your *biofield* (the silhouette of your physical body). It is spiraling around you from head to toe. You are now centered. At this time, you may choose to visually seal the silhouette of your body with your favorite color, in order to preserve your work.

You may also utilize this breathing visual as the first five minutes prior to any visualization piece, since you are also releasing tension and are therefore better prepared to successfully focus on the intention of your visualization work. Either way, you have created new oxygen for yourself, a very necessary element for your overall health.

Relaxation

Over Sea Over Sky

Transport yourself to a beach where the ocean is tranquil and translucent. It is daytime. Even though it is a sunny day, you can see a few clouds. One of the clouds begins to descend, until it arrives right by your side at shore. This cloud is there for you to use, as a flotation device. So you take a seat, and you begin to gently push it into the ocean. You may choose to lie on your stomach, and play with the water, or on your back, to admire the view. You watch the birds flying by. Relax, relax, relax. Pay attention to the sound of the waves as they splash against rocks. Inhale the clean and refreshing air. Now notice how the cloud you are lying on is beginning to rise with you in it. It is very safe and comforting, so you go with the flow. Before you know it, you are up in the sky, surrounded by other clouds. It is time to play and let loose. If you'd like, bounce from cloud to cloud; you are feeling very safe. The clouds feel like cashmere. Enjoy their softness and delicate treatment. Feel pampered.

Slowly feel as if you are beginning to descend with the cloud until you safely arrive at shore. Lie on the sand now, as all the clouds vanish and you are left with a bright-blue sky. Bathe in the sun. Feel the warmth and the love. You can stay here as long as you wish, and when you are ready, you can begin to bring your awareness back into your space by using your breath.

Come back to *Over Sea Over Sky* anytime. For now, preserve your relaxed state.

3. COMPLETING YOUR VISUALIZATION

When you have completed a visualization piece, it is just as important to use your breath to return your awareness to your body and space. Inhale and exhale as you focus and awaken each part of your body, starting from your head and going all the way down to your feet. When you open your eyes, take your time in standing up or beginning any activity. The deeper you go into your visualization, the more time you want to allow in order for your awareness and all your senses to fully return. If you have done a cleansing or healing visualization, make sure you create your protective shield immediately afterward (found in Part II, Section 8) to preserve the hard work you have completed. If you still feel you are in a daze, ground yourself by envisioning your feet solidly planted on the ground and a magnetic force keeping you grounded. Always remember to give thanks to whomever you invoked for assistance during the visualization. If you didn't invoke any divine entities, give thanks to your higher self. Don't forget to drink plenty of water.

PART II

Visualizations a la carte

1. MENTAL HEALTH

Reducing Anxiety

Anxiety is perhaps one of the most common issues presented in psychotherapy, and experiencing anxiety can be extremely draining and paralyzing. As with any emotional condition, it can be manifested in different forms. Some people become agitated and speak rather loudly and quickly. Others get very quiet and shaky. In an effort to assist patients who suffer from anxiety, many psychotherapists suggest that the patient uses relaxation techniques and learns how to breathe. You may have already concluded that I would suggest the same techniques. However, what I have found with patients suffering from anxiety is that if they do not expel whatever is causing the anxiety, the benefits of a relaxation exercise will be short lived, because they will still be holding on to the worry or issue that is making them anxious.

The technique I see the most success with in reducing or eliminating anxiety is that of *externalizing the symptoms*. This works because once the symptoms are outside of you, the battle will no longer be with yourself, and you will be able to see the symptoms with more clarity and begin to resolve them. Remember, *you* decide who is in control—the symptoms of anxiety or you. Here are a few examples you can follow to accomplish externalizing:

- Imagine you are watching yourself on a TV screen. An issue that causes you anxiety is taking place. Your physical self remains in front of the TV, holding a remote control. You have the choice to pause, fast forward, change the channel, lower the volume, or turn the TV off. This is how much control you have, and this is how clearly you see the issue now.

- Visualize yourself as the driver of your life. The symptoms from anxiety can ride on the back seat, and you can drop them off whenever you wish. You can also decide whether you allow them to ride with you at all.

• Envision a door that opens to your body. You can spot the symptoms of anxiety lining up to come inside. You can either welcome them and allow them to take over your body or you can shut the door before they can come in.

After you practice these externalizing visuals, then you can reap the benefits of a relaxation exercise, be it with more visualization or with breathing techniques.

Breaking Free from Depression

The Garden of Life

Imagine that you are standing right in front of a large glass window, where you can see the brightness of the day and the colors of a magnificent garden. There is a sign in the middle of this garden that has your name on it, and the sign is inviting you to join the garden. To make it easier, there is a small white bird that comes right to the window, and with its soft chirping, it lets you know that you will be safe. This bird will lead the way and will fly as slow or as fast, as high or as low, as you would like to go. So you dare to join the garden. Once you step out, you breathe in the fresh air and the aroma of the flowers surrounding you. *Ahhh!* It is so clean, so beautiful, so safe! Every step you take makes you realize what you have been missing. Every step you take, following the white bird, makes you want to join more and more.

So you decide to form a bouquet of flowers, and you carefully choose each flower with excitement. Once you form it, you realize its beauty, and you make yourself a gift of it. Now, allow yourself to go around dancing through the garden. If you would like, the bird can be your dancing partner. Feel alive. Feel the joy. Notice how easy it is to be a participant in life and how rewarding it is once you focus on what life has to offer.

Your spirit is alive! You deserve to live your life fully! Trust and dare to be part of the garden.

When you are ready, walk back towards the window, thanking the white bird for its lead and taking the bouquet of flowers you arranged as a reminder of this moment. Once back inside, remember that you can go into the garden whenever you are ready. Life is beautiful, and it is safe to join it.

Facing Claustrophobia

Claustrophobia is the fear of closed spaces and small places. As is the case with most anxiety disorders, most people who experience them will never admit to these issues in public. Yet this and all other anxiety-related disorders are unfortunately, extremely common. When someone is unable to control his or her fear, it can easily be manifested in the form of a panic attack.

With this particular phobia, I have used most of the senses to help you break through the fear. For instance, smell and taste can counteract the fear from fully forming and taking over the thoughts, since the fear of small places usually makes people feel queasy. Therefore, once you start creating a visual of something that breaks through the queasiness, you are home free. The same may be said about creating the feel of fresh air. It is soothing and calming.

Here are the claustrophobic situations commonly faced: being in a very small place, such as: a helicopter, an airplane, a crowded concert or sports event, a crowded subway, an MRI, or an elevator that is stuck.

See/Smell/Taste/Feel

Close your eyes and imagine you are cutting into a grapefruit (or a lemon or an orange). You begin to smell and then taste the grapefruit (or lemon or orange). It feels refreshing in your stomach, and hence, it settles it. Keep your eyes closed the entire time, if possible (hopefully someone is by your side to guide you through the crowd).

Now, think about fresh air and try to vividly feel the breeze on your face. Stay in this state as long as you can.

If you cannot close your eyes, pick a point of focus that gives you the illusion of space. Begin to design an outdoor setting on this point of focus. For instance, plant a tree and flowers. Then watch them grow. Remain occupied by choosing matching colors and envision yourself as a painter with a brush, creating this masterpiece. Add live beings to the scene. Bring in birds, butterflies, or even fairies.

Be playful and don't lose sight of your project until you are—done with the MRI, out of the helicopter or airplane, out of the stuck elevator, or out of the crowd. You get the picture. Be clever and overpower fear. You can do it. I know it because I have done this for myself, and it works.

Breaking Free from Panic Disorder

Panic attacks are delayed reactions to an accumulation of worries, fears, and stressors that no longer have a place within your physical self. I like to refer to this as a binge of unhealthy emotions. The antithesis of such is to learn to process and face your fears, in order to reduce your worries and stressors, so that your body and mind can be liberated together. Therefore, experiencing a panic attack is, in many ways, the purging of fears. You are externalizing the toxins you fed yourself with. We could say that a panic attack is a body's cry for help. It is saying, "I can't take this anymore!" All that has been held within needs to come out! You must then thank your body for letting you know its limits, by getting your attention in the form of a panic attack. If held within for too long and not manifested emotionally, it may later become a physical illness with far greater repercussions. Examples of these illnesses could be: indigestion, stomach ulcers, migraines and, even worse, cancer or a heart condition.

Now, anyone who has experienced a panic attack can verify that, while experiencing a panic attack, there is a tendency to forget to apply the tools learned to cope and reduce the intensity of the symptoms. One of the statements I use with my patients who suffer from panic disorder is "don't panic about the panic." However, I would prefer to help you with prevention rather than calming the storm once it has arrived.

Two of the most common situations for panic attacks to surface are: while driving in heavy traffic or while being in places with large groups of people (what is considered large may vary from person to person). This last example is also known as social phobia or agoraphobia. The aftermath of this phobia is usually a panic attack.

Following are two visualization pieces to be utilized as preventive measures. In other words, if you practice these visuals on a daily basis, you may reduce the intensity of your symptoms, reduce the duration of an episode and, in the long run, eliminate the experience of a panic attack altogether. Allow visualization to become the pleasant tool that frees you from the upsets of panic.

Sailing Through Traffic

> Prior to getting in the car, either as the driver or the passenger, tell yourself you are about to go sailing (as long as you like the ocean).

Imagine that your car is a boat, a very secure and comfortable one. The movement of the car is as smooth as the gentle waves of a calm body of water. The cars around you are other boats floating around. Slightly open your windows and focus on the breeze. How refreshing! How relaxing! As if on vacation, take it all in and enjoy the moment. It is a pleasant ride.

Take this visual with you and live through it when you are in the car. While still focusing on the road, you can make the ride be whatever you choose it to be.

The Box of Joy: Social Phobia/Agoraphobia

Imagine a time when you had a lot of fun in a social setting. Recall the laughter, the joy, the comfort. The last thought on your mind was leaving the setting, as you were enjoying yourself so very much. Now, create a treasure/joy box, either in physical form or through your imagination, and carry it with you wherever you go. In this box you will place all of the wonderful memories you have acquired from the pleasant social settings/experiences. Use all of your senses: the *feeling* of somebody's warm hug; then the pleasant *smells*—the fresh aroma of jasmine down a trail; the *sounds* of friendly laughter and friendly voices; the *taste* of your favorite appetizer or favorite drink; and the memory of the beautiful and inviting *sight*. If you are physically creating a joy box, write the memories, one statement at a time. You can open your joy box and take one of the statements out as an inspiration/motivation to keep you on plan (whether the plan is to go to the grocery store, a doctor's appointment, or a birthday party). Imagine, imagine, imagine. There are no limits. You can live and be free to do anything.

Enjoy yourself! Enjoy your life!

Additional Tips and Insights

While driving: If you are feeling the symptoms of panic starting to cripple you, start by telling yourself that you can always stop at the next exit. Once you reach the next exit, you can tell yourself you can keep going another minute. Keep expanding the time, minute by minute, and see how far you get without panic. You may surprise yourself.

While in social settings: Remember the saying "fake it till you make it"? Most actors imagine themselves in specific situations in order to deliver the most realistic portrayal of the character at hand. Actress Kim Basinger has publicly announced that she suffers from panic disorder, yet when she is in character, nobody could know the difference. Perhaps you can take an acting class for fun and break free from some of your restrictions. *Shh!* Nobody has to know how you make it happen.

Planning vs. Spontaneity

Most patients who I have worked with who suffer from panic disorder have confided that anticipation of a planned social event, or a trip that involves a long-distance drive, is conducive to worry, and they have often cancelled at the last minute. On the other hand, when there is a last-minute invitation, there is no room for overthinking or building up the anxiety associated with panic attacks. If you relate to this, ask your spouse, your family, and your close friends to surprise you with last-minute invites if they really want you to attend.

Eliminating Insomnia

Most people who experience insomnia have a completely exhausted body combined with a completely alert and saturated brain. Their thoughts keep them awake, and they do not know how to "turn the brain off." Another common reason for individuals experiencing insomnia is: high levels of physical pain. Again, it is their brain's focus on the pain that does not allow them to rest and go into sleep. Of course, there are other reasons for people to have insomnia, such as: consuming too much caffeine or other stimulants or the existence of a neurological condition.

Becoming aware of the main reason for your insomnia could be the first and most important step to recovery.

Allow me to share with you a few creative images with the goal of "shutting down the brain" and centering your thoughts on the beauty of sleep. Pick and choose from these ideas and use the one that best fits your mood for the night.

Erasing Thoughts

Imagine a white board. Everything that you are thinking is written on that board. Then imagine the words being erased, line by line, until the board is completely blank.

You Have the Key

> Get a sense that your thoughts are all entering a box, and once that box closes, those thoughts cannot go anywhere, because you hold the key. You decide when you want to open the box and reconnect with them. They will be there in the morning; just trust it to be so.

Conversion

> You can decide to convert your thoughts into anything else you wish—anything at all. For instance, transform them into a piece of your favorite cake and see yourself eating it. Transform them into a bouquet of flowers and enjoy the lovely scent through your imagination. Make believe your thoughts are butter and that the butter is under the sun and melting away.

You may also utilize the relaxation visual found in Part I, Section 2 to maximize your chances for a good night's sleep. If you do use the relaxation visual, you can certainly do so while lying in your bed.

As redundant as it may sound, once again—use your imagination. Only *you* know what works for you.

Healing Your Inner Child

Everyone has one or more painful memories from childhood. If not processed and healed, these memories may still be hindering your personal growth and power as an adult. As a psychotherapist, I have learned that once the adult self recognizes the need to save and love the inner child, the ability to move past the negative and painful memory is much more attainable. Hence, transformation takes place, and a stronger and more confident self emerges.

Here is one way to reach within and heal that inner child:

Connect with your instincts and allow them to bring up an age either when your most painful childhood memory begins or when it was felt the most. Start at as young an age as possible. Envision a bright-white light surrounding this young child until it becomes a safe bubble. This bubble will lift this child and transport him/her gently to a serene place. Allow the sun's rays to guide you. Travel as low or as high as you wish and arrive at either a familiar place or create one that feels safe. Once you arrive, you will find your adult self standing there. Walk towards your older self as you remove your younger self from the white bubble. It is safe now. The adult self can now care for the inner child by supporting him/her, protecting him/her, validating him/her, providing love and nurture, and acknowledging the deep wounds. Watch the younger self get older and older right in front of the adult and repeat the sequence of support, protection, validation, love, and nurture to as many ages and stages of your inner child as necessary until your

inner child grows to be exactly your present age.
Do the same to the adult self: support, protect,
validate, love, and nurture yourself. Embrace in
a warm hug until you integrate with each other
and become one again.

Keep this promise to yourself. Support. Protect.
Validate. Love and nurture *yourself.* Only then can
you heal. Only then can you transform and become
emotionally functional again.

Healing Past Trauma

Most human beings have experienced some form of
trauma during their lifetime. For some, a traumatic
event may not be considered as problematic as it
may by someone else. Nevertheless, if the experience
hindered you in any way, and you have yet to move
past it, it is indeed a trauma.

With my visualization CD titled *The Sacred OR*
(OR stands for operating room), you may be able to

go through all the layers of trauma and clear them with the aid of your divine entities. The CD can be purchased separately. For now, work with the following visualization to help you heal.

Clearing Your Heart

> Prepare to enter your heart. Envision yourself placing your hands over your heart. Notice how it externalizes and begins to grow, until it is much larger than your physical body. Ask for assistance from the divine (your guardian angel, God, an ancestor, a guide, your higher self, universal healing energy, etc.) on your journey to heal your heart from childhood traumas. Walk over one corner of your enlarged heart and notice a glass container by your feet. When you pick it up, you become instinctively aware that it is to be used to collect all pain as you begin to cleanse your heart. Slowly walk through your heart and use the power of your hands and the

assistance of the divine entities you requested to accompany you on this journey. Take your time. Breathe. You can do it. Feel empowered. It is time to give your heart a chance to start anew. Once you feel you have completed your cleansing process, hand the glass container to your divine entity, for them to seal and remove completely from your heart. Take a moment to sense your heart's color now. Use this time to sense other feelings: the kinder, lighter, easier feelings within. Allow the softness to take over your heart. Use your imagination to paint the interior of your heart "happy" (whatever "happy" may look like for you). Be happy. Be free from pain. You did it!

Now, walk back to the corner of your heart where you first entered. Thank the divine entity/ ies for their help as they disappear with the glass container. Watch how your heart begins to shrink in size until you are able to hold it in your hands and place it back over your chest. It instantly integrates into your body. Breathe. Breathe. Breathe. Give thanks. Give thanks. Give thanks.

Releasing Fears

Untangling

Close your eyes and connect with your body by simply focusing on it. Without questioning your instincts, get a sense of where your fears are stored within you—go with your first answer. Now envision the fears taking the physical form of a tangled necklace. Slowly envision yourself holding the necklace and patiently untangling it. Take your time. You will get through it. When it's fully untangled, use white light to make this necklace slowly vanish. Breathe deeply and exhale.

Get a sense of your body again, now free from the tangled necklace (fears). Notice how clear it seems and how much lighter it feels. Remind yourself that you have the power to release your fears completely. This is a choice you make. Have patience with yourself and trust yourself. You are free.

Pain Management

The body is quite intelligent. We cannot escape from its warnings. When physical pain is activated without any apparent accident or known disease, we begin to wonder and many times panic about what it might be. Pain is a critical signal sent to you from your body after you have been unaware of other subtle signals, such as mild headaches or tiredness that, again, have come about without any apparent reason. If after going to your doctor you are left with no answers other than "there is nothing wrong with you," then perhaps your body signals are cries for help. Maybe you need to learn to slow down or take better care of yourself.

There is nothing more powerful than using your breath to release pain. Breathing is a way of recycling oxygen. Therefore, with every inhalation and every exhalation you are restoring yourself anew.

Visualizations

1> As you connect with your breath, take an inventory of your entire body, one area at a time. When breathing into a specific area of your body, imagine that you are vacuuming away all its pain and discomfort with your inhalation and that as you exhale you are releasing all that has been vacuumed outside of your space. Continue practicing this breathing exercise until you have worked with every part of your body, including the parts of your body that you do not feel need to be restored. (If your pain is based on emotional captivity, it will travel from one part of the body to another rather than leaving your body completely. Therefore, it is imperative to work on your entire body).

2> Another visual or style to utilize while working with your breath to reduce pain is to consider your breath as localized anesthesia. Follow the breathing pattern from number 1, but instead of getting a sense of a vacuum, simply send warm energy to the parts of your body that are in most pain, by inhaling and exhaling directly onto them. Keep the focus on those parts of your body for as long as you need to. And, of course, if you have religious/spiritual beliefs, invoke the presence of the divine entities you have faith in, and watch them/feel them as they heal and send love to your body. Don't forget to give thanks to the divine entities as well as to your higher self.

Some of my patients who follow these simple techniques have told me that they experience relief sometimes lasting up to seventy-two hours. Some experience 100 percent relief. Measure your level of pain before you begin breathing (on a scale of zero to ten, with ten being the worst your pain can be), and then take note of it again immediately after you do your breathing work. Use what you have (your breath) to naturally heal—one day at a time.

2. DAY-BY-DAY ISSUES

Starting Your Day with Intention

Beginning your day with the right intentions leads to focus, clarity and, inevitably, manifestation.

Sitting in an upright position with your legs folded in a pretzel, place your hands in prayer position close to your heart, and with your eyes closed, look up to your third eye (the point between your eyebrows).

Breathe slowly at first and then begin to take deeper breaths. Sense that your body is connected firmly to the ground and simultaneously sense your connection from above, as if you have a string attached from your head up to the sun. At the center of it all, and right in front of you, is your day—today. Combine your needs and wants for the day, and bring them close to your heart. Say out loud, "Today I intend to _____." Watch a ball of energy unfold and spread out evenly throughout your day, setting everything in its perfect place at the perfect moment. Feel your heart at ease and trust that everything will work out ideally today. Breathe and integrate yourself into your day. Give thanks.

Creativity

The Earth is Your Canvas

Imagine the possibilities! Imagine our earth as a blank canvas, ready to take on whichever shape, color, size, or scent you desire. Find yourself standing in front of this empty and clean earth. Envision your body larger than the earth itself. Connect with your fingertips. On them you will sense oil paint. Focus on one corner of the earth at a time, and allow your fingers to "do the magic." Be as conservative or as liberal as you wish to be. This is *your* canvas! This is *your* earth! Create, create, create! Use your body's movement as well to form shapes. Dance around. Giggle. Take your time to complete your vision. Now, take a very close look at what *you* have done. You have created *your* earth by going with your own rhythm and pace. How powerful you are! It is pretty spectacular, isn't it? Now step onto *your* world and create for today. The magic is literally at your fingertips.

Focus

Ah, the beauty of nature! Oh, there is so much to see, so much to listen to, so much to explore! Yet, in order to truly enjoy it all, we must give our undivided attention to one aspect of it at a time. If I had to write a paper to describe one specific tree, I could not allow myself to be distracted by anything else. So let's imagine precisely that.

Let us focus on this one tall and ancient tree and describe it the best we can. We will go from top to bottom. The tree seems so tall! I will guess it is about thirty feet tall. Its foliage is very full and flamboyant, and it has branches that extend about fifteen feet to each side. Its leaves appear shiny and intact. There are too many leaves to imagine counting, and they are very small in size. We touch one leaf, and it seems almost slippery-soft. As we look closer, we begin to notice the trunk, with layers and layers that appear ready to peel off. We allow our eyes to move now from the middle of the trunk to the roots of the tree. Wow! What a spectacular sight! The roots seem about five feet long, and their protuberance is quite admirable. We walk over the roots as a child would, with our arms extended to the sides as we try to balance our bodies from one end of the roots to the other. What a ride!

You did it! You only need to show interest in the task at hand and explore its details with childlike curiosity. Before you know it, you will be deeply immersed in your project, and your task will be completed. Enjoy the process!

Patience

There is a popular saying: "patience is a virtue." I would say that patience is not a quality but rather a gift that we choose to give ourselves. Life happens at our own pace, based on our thought patterns and our intentions. Some people are able to set fabulous intentions—yet they cannot master the ability to let the intention go and allow things to happen when the moment is just right. This doesn't mean that we have to wait forever or that life isn't happening at our own pace. What this means is that the more we focus on timing, the more energetic pressure we deliver—hence, the longer things will take to manifest.

Additionally, if we can think of the process between planting a seed and the time it takes to harvest, we may become extremely impatient. We recognize that it takes time, love, and dedication before we have the final product in hand. However, if we can focus on the miraculous *process*, and concentrate on one aspect of the process at a time, we can then celebrate the short-term goals. We can say "I see a little stem coming out of the ground!" instead of "It's just a stem—who knows how much longer it's going to take to harvest?" There is an indescribable sense of joy when we experience the process. Most of life happens to be a process. We get excited about a certain event—be it a wedding, a graduation, or a relocation—yet the event itself may take four hours, while the preparation may have taken us years. If we do not allow ourselves to enjoy the process, we are simply missing out on life.

Transport yourself with these visuals:

You are in your backyard, or on any fertile ground you consider warm and promising. You are holding a very special seed in your hands. It is called *the seed of patience.* Choose the perfect ground spot for it, and before you plant it, set the intention, bless it, and give thanks in advance for its promise. For example, you might say, "By planting the seed of patience, I intend to manifest a joy for the process. I ask that God bless it and my heart bless it with love and excitement. I give thanks to you, seed of patience, for everything you give me and will forever give me." Now carefully plant your seed. This very moment is the most precious to enjoy as you feel the cold sensation of the soil in your hands and the texture of small rocks, worms, and mud. Press the seed deeply into the soil that you've selected for it to grow in.

Water it. Feel the dirt between your fingernails and smell the moisture. Watch as the sun's rays caress the ground and again give thanks to the process. Have fun going out every day to water this seed and allow it to surprise you—with a stem, then a trunk, a branch and, finally, your fruit. Do you see how much fun it can be? Join in with the miracle of life. Patience is your gift to yourself.

Motivation/Courage

When I was six years old, I was getting ready to perform a song in front of about five hundred people. As my mother was combing my hair, she looked at me in the mirror and advised me: "When you go on stage, just pretend you are singing right here, just for me. You can do anything." Whenever I feel as if I need motivation and courage, I recall that moment with my mother, and I go about my business with the utmost confidence.

In my opinion, there is nothing more motivating than listening to encouraging words from that one person who inspires you the most.

Cheers

You see yourself waking up to the sound of your favorite song. You get out of bed, already in a great mood, and begin to dance to the rhythm of your song. As you are getting ready to go out, you receive a phone call from your favorite person, the one that motivates you the most. He or she is calling you to wish you luck and give you some last words of encouragement before your big moment: "You are one of a kind; you are going to do a fantastic job; you are the best at what you do; of course you can do it!"

Your heart is now filled with enthusiasm. You take a few moments to daydream about how your performance will turn out. You see everyone extremely interested in what you have to say or do. Watch yourself as your task becomes effortless. You hear the cheers from your team: "Bravo! Terrific job!" Stay focused and make this dream become a reality.

Slowing Down

The Hammock

Blue skies, bright sunshine, and a nice breeze make for an absolutely perfect day. You are at the beach, and you are walking towards two palm trees. Right between them you find a lovely hammock. It has been waiting for you, so you sit on it and then slowly melt right into it. It is so comforting and relaxing. Let the breeze swing you back and forth until you find yourself at complete ease.

Without needing to leave your comfortable hammock, you see a piece of paper. This piece of paper can register your thoughts without you having to write them down, and once the thoughts are registered on that piece of paper, they will no longer interfere with your day. Use this time to list all your worries and to-dos, and send them to register on the piece of paper simply by thinking of them. As you register them one by one, you begin to feel lighter. Your to-dos are being organized and prioritized as you set them all down on paper. Now, allow yourself to genuinely relax and be certain that everything will get done. Know that worrying about it or constantly reviewing it will not make it any easier.

The hammock continues to swing back and forth, while you enjoy and prolong this feeling of ease for as long as you wish. It *is* that easy. You deserve to gift yourself with ease.

Ready for Bed

A good night's sleep is precious in more than one way. It restores our bodily cells, recharges us, and resets our minds. The amount of rest needed to replenish the body varies from person to person. In today's world, most of us reduce the number of hours we sleep per night in order to complete our to-do-lists for the day. Precisely because we live in an era of busy schedules and many stressors, we must learn to love and protect our sleep time.

Your sleep represents time for you as well as a reward for all your hard work. Start respecting it and watch how it works for you in the long run. Create rituals and a sacred space prior to your sleep time:

- Take a warm bath with Epsom salt or aromatherapy scents.
- Drink a chamomile tea or a lemon-and-honey tea.

- Create an environment of peace and quiet (that is, avoid watching the news or any other distressing program).

- Adjust the room temperature to your liking.

- Create a calming scent via scented candles or incense.

- Write down your to-do list for tomorrow to remove it from your thoughts.

Visualize

When you are already in bed, imagine a pool full of cotton. Immerse yourself in it and allow your body to float on the cotton. Your body is being caressed and pampered by delicate softness no matter in what direction it turns. Treat yourself with this kind of gentleness and enjoy a soothing night's sleep. Sweet dreams.

3. LIFE TRANSITIONS

Facing Change

Most individuals will experience a mixture of emotions when they are facing change. Some will describe their experience as mainly exciting, especially if it is a planned and voluntary change. Yet there will always be an underlying feeling of fear, simply because most human beings form attachments that keep them feeling safe. When there is change ahead, the brain registers this as a red alert, and the heart automatically translates this into unsafe territory, thereby instilling fear. For those who experience involuntary changes, such as a job loss and having to start work somewhere new, or moving into a new house because they could no longer afford the old one, the sense of fear will dominate. Most people will agree that, at some point in their lives, they have thought about running away from their problems—just moving away, or leaving a current relationship or job. Yet, in the end, the problem goes with them, wherever they choose to escape. What we are trying to do here is the opposite. We are working towards releasing our fears so that we are then able to recreate a sense of safety wherever we are. Hence, healthier selves will inevitably emerge as we focus on releasing and recreating.

Following is a visualization that focuses on releasing fears, replacing those fears with excitement, and creating ourselves anew.

It is Safe to Face Change

Watch yourself sitting still, right in the middle of your life. Literally watch yourself sitting in a meditative state, say, in the middle of your house, or in the middle of your office, or in the middle of the town that you currently live in. Feel the energy of the earth below you as it supports your physical body and then feel the energy of the sun as it draws you above. Feel your physical body being raised as if you were levitating. Consciously leave behind any attachments to the space you are moving from; imagine light beams coming out of your tailbone. Simultaneously, bring with you the "feel-good" memories. Recognize that you have the choice of releasing the fears and that you can take with you a sense of safety wherever you go.

Now, get a sense of a stronger connection with the energy of the sun and feel the strength of its rays. If you can externalize your vision from yourself, watch your physical body glowing as it is levitating in space. Allow the energy of the sun to wrap around you and feel the warmth and safety it brings. Travel to your new location (home, office, relationship, community, etc.). If you do not know what this new situation looks like, this is your time to create it from scratch. Then slowly watch your body arriving from above and sitting down right in the middle of your new place/situation. Consciously connect with your heart and allow it to spread warmth and love into that new space or relationship. Externalize yourself from your physical body again and watch yourself as if you were already living there and/or working there, etc. Let it play out as your ideal self would. Experience it happening right now, and register details.

Slowly bring yourself back into your physical body, making a conscious choice to remember the details and to feel the excitement of this new adventure. This is your chance to recreate your life, and make it even better. Embrace this opportunity and give thanks.

New Beginnings

I strongly believe that the most difficult aspect of getting yourself to begin anew is your entangled connection with the old—the habits. What is familiar to you becomes your norm, even if it is dysfunctional.

In order to experience a new beginning, I feel you must have a clean slate, a complete disconnection from the old. This will allow you to set yourself free to venture and, most importantly, to get excited about the new beginning—this is the opposite of fearing it. I have created the following visual to assist you with this process.

Starting Anew

> Envision yourself, your body and spirit, completely present and connected to life as you know it. Now, get a sense that your body is literally plugged into an energy field, which keeps you perceiving your life as it presently is.

All you need to do is unplug yourself from that energy field to feel free and hence, to start anew. If you need divine assistance, just ask. Your angels, ascended masters, and ancestors are there to aid you anytime you wish. The key is to ask for help. Sense the unplugging taking place easily and effortlessly. Now feel your body so loose and light that you can do somersaults and pirouettes in the air. Fly around if you wish. Combine color and a feel to this new space. It is nothing but freeing and promising. Start this very moment to enjoy the clear path. Create a palette of new colors that help you align with your new beginning and immerse your body into these colors. How spectacular is what you have created!

Go out there and embrace your new beginning with excitement. Nothing can stop you now!

Clearing Illness

It is my understanding that physical illness derives from unexpressed emotions. To be *e-motion-all* equates to taking action on a feeling. When *e-motions* are not set *in motion*, they quickly begin to build up within our bodies, until they hit a point of no return. The explosion is then inevitable, and it can take the form of anger, a panic attack, or a physical illness. Let us visualize healing our bodies and ourselves through faith and self-love.

Healing Through Faith and Self-Love

> Envision a crystal clear drop of water coming down from the heavens and gently falling right above your head. This drop of water is pure and cleansing. Invite it to come inside and allow it to travel from the top of your head and go slowly right through you: passing through your brain, your eyes, your nose, your throat, and

then all the way through your chest and your heart. It cleanses and purifies every inch within you, all your organs and cells. Say a prayer of your choice as you go through this cleansing process, until the drop of water reaches your feet and it evaporates completely. Breathe in and out as you connect with your renewed body and welcome health and balance into it.

Now, imagine two large, exquisite white angel wings wrapping your body completely from back to front. The angel wings are giving your body warmth, love, and compassion. Embrace this pure love from above and connect with your own self-love. Feel the power of this omnipotent love taking over and healing your body as you heal yourself from unexpressed emotions. Allow the tears to help. Release and believe!

Gift yourself daily with self-love, even if it's only one drop of water at a time. You deserve to be healthy.

Loss and Mourning

Loss reminds us of our mortality, and thus, it brings up fears, sadness, anger, and anxiety—simply because we do not have control over the outcome. Hence, we strive for peace, for closure, and ultimately, acceptance. Yet, there are many stages people experience prior to reaching the final goal of acceptance. In the beginning, for most people, one of the main goals is to find out how their deceased loved one is doing, if at all possible. It's common for me to receive this request when working with clients who are in the beginning stages of their mourning. "I just want to know that he is okay," they will say, or "If only I could speak to him one more time."

Through visualization, I help them transport themselves and achieve the connection with their recently passed loved one. By sharing the following visualization, I hope I can help you, too, in connecting with your deceased loved ones.

Connecting Again

> Allow the stillness of time and space to be revealed to you by using your breath and clearing your thoughts completely. Release all expectations. Simply be. Now visualize yourself as you externalize your spirit from your body—it's as if a bright light is sweeping you from the bottom of your feet all the way up to your head. Watch that light as it rapidly transports itself and becomes a small dot of light. It can travel anywhere. Find yourself—a light spirit—in a galaxy of bright stars and slowly feel the energetic pull towards one particular star. This light will guide you into a private and cozy corner where it can reveal itself to you. Follow, and as you get closer, notice the light softening and transforming into the body

and shape of the person whom you are seeking to connect with. You are also transformed back into your physical body, and you can both feel each other's presence. Get as close as you wish and place one hand over your heart. Anything and everything you would like to say or ask of this being can be heard within your heart. Take your time. Open yourself to feel any sensations of touch and embrace them fully. Allow these feelings to be imprinted within your heart, keeping them within reach for any other time you might wish to connect with your deceased loved one.

Exchange your final words and thank him/her for being present and willing to connect with you. Thank your spirit for leading you. Keeping your hand over your heart, become a light again and watch your loved one also become light once more, as he/she travels through the galaxy. You travel back to earth, bringing with you a sense of peace and a certainty that you may connect with your loved one anytime, as this visualization guides you to. Return to your physical body and give thanks to your spirit once again. Breathe deeply and awaken every part of you.

May God bless your heart and continue to bring you peace and comfort during this sorrowful phase of your life.

Celebrating Life

It's your birthday! This day marks *your* New Year's celebration. How you welcome this day and how you celebrate it can influence the vibration of your entire year.

There are many cultures that have established and followed rituals for the New Year's celebration. I suggest that you also create a special ritual to celebrate your day, regardless of your age. In addition to the traditional rituals established, like singing happy birthday while you blow out candles and make a wish, here are some other examples. Your new ritual could be an offer to nature, such as throwing a rose into the ocean or planting a tree in your backyard. It could be an offering to God, such as a white candle and a prayer. Whichever ritual you choose should come from the heart. Your rituals can change from year to year or from decade to decade. You will know what to do if you follow your heart. In the meantime, use the following visualization to enhance and solidify the celebration of *your* life.

Happy Birthday to Me!

> Bring yourself to imagine you are going for a ride in a car that can travel through time. There is a large sign at the entrance of a road; it reads "My Life." You know this refers to you, and you first notice a billboard with a picture of yourself during the happiest moment of your

life thus far. As you drive, you begin to travel through the different accomplishments you have achieved throughout your life. You are watching them as a spectator. You travel through the times when others have cheered and celebrated you. No event is too small. You continue this ride and realize how much there is about you that needs to be celebrated and how important your life truly is. At the end of the road there is another billboard with flashing lights, that reads "Happy Birthday to Me! I celebrate my life with pride, and I look forward to another year full of opportunities for me to be the best I can be. Life is worth celebrating!"

4. RELATIONSHIPS

New Relationship

Ahhh! There is nothing more pure and exciting than the beginning of a relationship. This applies regardless of the nature of this new relationship. The curiosity . . . the possibilities . . . the unfolding of togetherness . . .

Following is a visualization piece to use alone or with this new person. Remember, this new relationship can be a romantic one, but it can also apply to a new friendship or even a newborn in your life. We are all one. We are all connected. Therefore, bringing awareness and purpose to a new relationship can help enhance its beauty.

Caterpillars Unite

Find yourself staring at nature, specifically, the very fertile soil in the middle of a forest.

There are tall, ancient trees all around you. As you closely look into the ground, you can see a caterpillar finding its way. However you can envision this, set the intention to become this caterpillar. Get used to its body and its "dance." Become aware of your surroundings with even more precision as you begin to sense the proximity of another caterpillar. Feel the excitement rushing through the body. It gets closer and closer, until you are face to face. No words are necessary, only a sense of connection and belonging. The magic is there. All you need to do is touch. Once you've touched, notice how both of you caterpillars are ready to transform into butterflies—except that this time, instead of two separate butterflies, you both become one giant, unique, and ever-so-happy butterfly. Watch the color formation. Sense your wings spreading. Fly around for the first time, sensing the beauty of your union, and begin to set intentions about how you want this union to develop as you find yourself become stronger and more confident. You have now become one. Embrace the beautiful butterfly you have both created and bring out the best from within each other—the butterfly that you both are.

Getting Married

Throughout time, the sacred institution of marriage has taken many shapes and forms. Regardless, it is and will always be a union of two individuals who choose to be together and start their own family. It is a time of hope and possibility. It is a time for celebration. Whether you have a strong belief system or none at all, rituals and faith become important in the shaping of this bond.

I would like to propose a few rituals in the form of visualizations, to assist you in solidifying your togetherness.

1> Sit together under your favorite tree or by the beach. Holding hands, close your eyes and begin to narrate, with lots of detail, how you foresee your future together. Begin with your wedding day. Take turns while sharing. The easiest approach to this is to imagine you are telling each other stories you already know. Let the stories flow, allowing the subconscious to take over. Keep your eyes closed the entire time. The more details you provide, the more exciting it gets. You can describe how the kiss after the "I-dos" feels. Have fun! Describe what the guests look like and who is the best dancer. In the same manner, visualize every corner of your home and give each other a play by play of what a day in your lives is like. Daydream about children, about getting along while discussing finances, and about compromising on the major decisions within your life. You may be surprised at the many similarities in your daydreams. Immediately after your daydreaming narratives, write these experiences down, as if you are creating the book of your lives together. You can also choose to write a book for every decade prior to physically experiencing those years. Additionally, you can also create a picture collage of what you envision your marriage to be. This approach will allow very little room for doubt. Manifestation will then be inevitable.

2> Envision a giant gold ring crowning the two of you together. Its light shines all around you and all the way down to your feet. As you walk through life, keep the visual of that giant gold ring above you. You will always feel that you are together, even if one of you is not physically present. This is your golden circle. It is sacred. Give it a name. The only ones that can enter this circle are the two of you and, later on, your children.

3> The same love you give to each other is also necessary for the space you share. Shower your home with love. Do this together. You can create a phrase that you say out loud to and in your space every day, as if you were talking to a live being. "You are the best! We love you so much! Thank you for being so bright and comforting!" Your space will hold that love for you and support you when you most need it.

Facing Challenges within Relationships

Relationships are far from perfect. Since relationships involve more than one person, it is a given that you will encounter challenges and differences. The effort you place in making the relationship work may depend on your commitment to that other person.

Maintaining a healthy relationship requires dedication and work from both individuals. However, when the going gets tough, many people tend to give up and move on. In some cases, moving on may be necessary, as it is equally important to recognize when the differences are too large to repair or when the lessons within the difficult experiences have been learned and outgrown. Hence, the following suggested visual is about helping you recognize the lessons within your differences, in order to determine whether you should part from the relationship or make amends and grow even stronger together.

Recognizing the Lessons

> Begin by watching yourself climb a tree and continue until you reach its top. The tree is very broad and comfortable enough to support you as you sit on top of it. You now have a clear view of your life. On the far left you will see yourself in a scene with one or both of your parents. Do

not force this to happen, but rather allow some memory of you with your parents to come up that represents a struggle or a difference in opinion. Determine the theme of that issue and watch how you handled it back then.

Remove your attention from that scene and now look straight ahead. You will now encounter a scene with you and another person who represented a significant relationship from the past. In the same way as you did with the prior scene, allow a memory to surface where you and this significant other were experiencing a challenging moment within your relationship. Watch carefully to grasp how you handled the issue and determine the theme of that issue as well.

Now move your focus to the far right and this time, bring about the issue you are facing within your present relationship. Pay close attention to how you are handling this challenging issue and determine whether there are any similarities with the memories you just revisited. Now imagine yourself handling this issue with your partner in a different, perhaps more amenable, way. Play out a scene where both of you are clear about deciding how to proceed with the relationship. Remember, however, that one can only change oneself. Even though the lessons within the relationship are for both of you, these lessons can certainly be different for you and for the other person involved. Try to be honest. Ask yourself, "Am I willing to take responsibility for my choices and actions? Can I recognize a pattern within my relationships that needs to be healed and cleared in order for me to have healthier relationships from this point on?" Then, you decide. It will always involve work, but you will reap the benefits for life as you create a smoother path for this and all future relationships.

Slowly climb down from the tree and settle your feet on the ground. Use your breath to fully return and grab a pen and paper to write down what you have learned about yourself.

May growth and happiness be with you.

5. Our Relationship with Food

Our most recent generations seem to place a tremendous amount of pressure on what our bodies and ideal weight should be. Being thin, or even underweight, appears to be applauded, labeled as most aesthetically pleasing, and synonymous with health and success. Unlike in the past, this issue has transcended genders. It used to be that females felt most of the pressure to be slender, but now men feel this pressure just as much. This creates a sense of competition among teens and the early development of eating disorders, obsessive-compulsive disorder, low self-esteem, depression, and anxiety. The need to control food becomes an obsession for many. Some overcome it, and some end up living their entire lives with eating disorders or the disorders associated with the need to control food.

The Healthy Dimension

Only food can provide the necessary nutrients to keep our bodies functional and healthy. Bodies come in all shapes and sizes. We seem to forget this. Rather than focusing on cravings or what the ideal body shape and size should be, the following visualization is designed to help you take food at its face value and remind yourself daily that your choices in food will either nourish your body or harm it in the long run. Let us focus on what really matters: feeling physically healthy and accepting and loving ourselves unconditionally.

Your Health is Beautiful

As you utilize your breath to center yourself, also envision your body levitating until it slowly moves past the sky. When you touch the sky, you are physically able to move past what your eyes are used to seeing. You find yourself crossing into another dimension, leaving behind everything you know to be true, and opening yourself to a new reality.

As your feet touch the ground, notice that it happens to be purple. It feels very warm and loving. You begin to take an inventory of your surroundings. You are able to see brighter and foreign colors in nature. You become curious and take walks to explore these new elements of nature. With every step you take, you realize that your feet have roots into these grounds. Just like the trees and plants, your body also grows and is nourished from these grounds. You are part of this magic. You are part of this health. Choose fruits and vegetables that appeal to you and watch the reflection of your body through the sunrays and any bodies of water you find on your path. Also, be attentive to how your body feels once it has consumed these foods. Decide when your body is satisfied and leave some of the foods for later or for tomorrow. As you consume these natural foods, your body brightens and looks happier and healthier. And since you are connected and, therefore, a part of these grounds, you are simultaneously participating in adding beauty to the panorama. You are beautiful! Your body is a reflection of what you consume. If you make healthy choices, your body will return the favor by prolonging its life and its vitality. See yourself as ageless and look around you one last time, as you notice other beings in all different shapes and sizes. Yet what seems to matter the most is their brightness and being in harmony with the panorama.

Take a mental and emotional picture of this dimension and as you slowly return to the space that we live in, remember what matters most: physical health, full self-acceptance, and self-love. It's all relative to the reality you choose to embrace.

Slowly connect with your breath again and begin to descend onto your space. Ground yourself and awaken to the reality you feel best in. Have a healthy day.

6. THE PROCESS OF PROCREATION

Infertility and Miscarriage

One of the most rewarding life experiences for human beings, if not the most rewarding, is to procreate. In the same way, one of the most heartbreaking experiences for a couple is to face infertility issues; sometimes these are explainable and sometimes not. I have taken this issue very seriously as a psychotherapist, and during my research on finding methods to help others emotionally through this process, I came across energy psychology. I learned about how much of the unexplained infertility issues are directly associated with emotional blockages within our energy centers and meridians. Since then, I have worked with many women (and men, as the male's emotional blockages will affect the process just as much as a low sperm count will) to break free from these negative ties and help them conceive a child.

There are many women who will experience miscarriages as well. The trauma of this loss is indescribable. It is a time when a woman will feel very lonely; this is not something that we openly share with others. The spouse will be sad, but because the woman was the one carrying the baby and already experiencing body changes, her sadness will be that much more enhanced.

Once a woman or a couple has experienced any of these issues and then become successfully pregnant, there is the tendency to be fearful throughout the pregnancy, given the prior loss and physical and emotional hurdles they've experienced.

Visualization aids in staying focused on your goal to have a child, as this can be a lengthy process, and patience and faith run out very quickly. Visualization will also aid in remaining at peace, gaining patience, and keeping the faith. As with all other things, manifestation takes place only when we *believe* it to be possible.

Following is a visualization piece to positively contribute to the different aspects described above: the waiting, the devastation from a miscarriage, and the challenges of pregnancy itself.

Keeping the Faith

After centering yourself with your breath, find yourself visually lying down on green grass in the middle of a very fertile field. It is sunrise time, and you have the entire view to yourself. You cannot help but look around and notice the effect this sunrise has on nature. The flowers begin to open, the leaves perk up, and the colors seem brighter and much more alive. Extend your hands, your feet, and then your entire body to the sun and find yourself having the same experience as nature. You begin to shine and blossom. You begin to heal from any physical or emotional blocks you have experienced while trying to conceive a child. Through the sun's rays, you notice the presence of an almighty (God, source, universal healing energy—whichever your belief system might be), which comes to pick you up and cradle you. You feel protected, cared for, loved, attended, and healed. Connect with your heart and feel your faith and patience growing. Tell yourself out loud, "Whatever it takes, I will not give up on my dream to procreate and bring a healthy baby into this world. I deserve it. I am open to it, and I allow the timing of God and the readiness of the child's soul to come to me, to my family."

Watch as your entire physical body changes colors as a sign of transformation. Express your gratitude to God and watch as the presence becomes wrapped up in the sun. Connect with your breath once again as you slowly bring yourself back into your physical space. Trust, be patient, believe, and remain focused on this precious goal.

Pregnancy

I spent over five years daydreaming about getting pregnant and having a healthy and loving child of my own. Regardless of the disappointments and heartaches that came from my lost pregnancies and/or my unsuccessful attempts to conceive, I kept the vision intact: "I will be a Mom in this lifetime, and I will procreate a child of my own flesh."

When my son was about two months away from being manifested in my womb, I began experiencing dreams in which he would be talking to me. He introduced himself as Sebastian, and I knew that I had to name him Sebastian. Obviously, I also knew it would be a boy. Of course, because of the many miscarriages and disappointments I'd endured—even though my pregnancy had been confirmed and I had heard his heartbeat at the doctor's office—there was a part of me that was fearful of embracing this reality. I thought it would not last, that this pregnancy would become another loss. I had to work very hard at releasing those past experiences in order to fully welcome this one: a full-term pregnancy.

I would like to share with you a few visuals that helped me embrace the pregnancy and safeguard the baby throughout it. Use one or use them all at once. And above all, have fun with them. Your baby will feel it as you transmit your energy and intention to him/her. My son is full proof of this, as he is the most determined child I have ever known, and I was nothing but determined before and during the pregnancy.

Sending Love

> Bring up a picture or a memory of a place and time when you felt love at its purest. Get a sense that your entire body and energy field are being charged with this pure love. Welcome it, and feel it penetrate through all your pores.

Now, pay close attention to your navel, and allow all of this pure love to be concentrated at your navel and travel through the umbilical cord until it reaches your baby's heart. Charge him/her entirely with this love. Imagine you can see him/her smiling. Now create a shell of light (using gold or white), and seal this pure and perfect love. If you can imagine your baby being a pearl and your body being the shell, watch as the shell seals and protects your pearl. Use this visual anytime you want to reconnect with your baby, even if it is by sending verbal messages. He /she will surely receive them.

Protection

Anytime you are about to interact with others, envision the womb surrounded by a cocoon with the colors of the rainbow.

Listening to Your Baby's Messages

> If the baby starts moving or kicking you while
> you are surrounded by others, ask him/her to
> send you a clear message of what he/she needs
> or wants by using the vibration of the umbilical
> cord. Close your eyes, and listen to your heart.
> Your instincts will tell you what your baby said.
> This can also be used during the infant months
> when your baby cannot use words yet.

They say that mothers always know how to interpret a baby's cry and determine his/her needs. However, as a therapist, I have encountered many moms who feel at a loss. I believe these moms do not trust their instincts; therefore, they miss and doubt the messages. Remember, the first hunch is always the right one.

Connecting with Your Unborn Child's Soul

Ever wonder what your baby's personality will be like? Are you eager to feel and see your baby and ask as many questions as you can? I believe in and have guided many couples through visualizations intended to connect with an unborn child's soul. These visualizations are always full of messages and confirmations for the parents-to-be. This is possible because a soul is eternal and timeless. An unborn child's soul has already picked you as his/her parents because he/she feels you align with his/her lifetime purpose.

In addition, during pregnancy and infancy it is very common for fathers to feel left out. The focus is either on the mother-to-be, the baby, or both. Hence, the following visualization piece is not only intended to connect with the soul of the unborn child but also to establish a family bond and bring purpose to the roles of each parent-to-be. If you can, practice this visualization piece in the room you have designated for your soon-to-arrive baby. Sitting and facing each other, extend one hand to each other and hold hands. Place the other hand on the belly of the mother-to-be.

Find His/Her Star

Imagine you will be taking a boat ride together, Mom-and-Dad-to-be. You arrive at a beautiful lake at nighttime and are exposed to a clear sky full of bright stars. You begin to sail through this tranquil lake until you find a spot where you want to rest and admire the stars. When you arrive, you both lie on your backs and begin to pay close attention to the shining stars. Yet now you have a mission: you are both looking out for that star or stars that sparkle the most. You are looking for the star or stars that connect with you; the star or stars that want to speak with you. You begin to notice this star or stars slowly making their way down towards you. As it/they do, it/they start to take the shape of a person/ child, or perhaps just the face of a person. If you are unable to see a face or person, pay attention to the sounds, and listen to what this star or stars have to say. This star/these stars are the stars of your child/children to come. Ask them questions, or simply listen with your heart to what they have to say. Officially welcome them into your lives, and also take time to let them know how excited you feel about their arrival and about them choosing you as their parents. If it feels right and you have spiritual beliefs, invite God, the angels, or anything you believe in to participate in this experience. Energetically embrace in a warm hug as you exchange the love within your hearts. Give thanks for their willingness to communicate with you, and tell them you will see them very soon. Slowly watch the star or stars be carried by the divine entity you invited, until you see them rise up and join the rest of the stars. Now place your hands on each others' hearts. Watch as you sit and begin to sail back to shore. Slowly make your way back into your baby's room, and when you open

your eyes, embrace in a hug.

Share with each other what you saw and felt. You may

be surprised at how similar your experiences were.

7. ABUNDANCE

Manifesting More:
Money, Love, Joy, Friendship, Health

For the past few decades, it appears that people have equated abundance exclusively with money. However, when referring to abundance, my intention is to include anything and everything that can flow and grow in our lives. Therefore, we can create a list of numerous things, such as: joy, love, health, awareness, and friendships—you name it.

When we come from a place of desperation and anxiety, we delay the arrival of abundance. Therefore, it is crucial to work with releasing those fear-based feelings (use the visualization on releasing fears found in Part II, Section 1). What we need to do is focus on gratitude. How lovely it is to hear someone say, "I am grateful for being abundantly gifted with health! I have and cherish my abundance of love." By now you should understand that making a statement that comes from gratefulness sets an easier path towards manifesting what you visualize. This is so, simply because it comes from the heart. You must genuinely feel grateful in order to "place the order" into the universe and receive your "package." That is, your desires for more abundance can only be fulfilled once you humbly embrace what you already have (as little as you think it might be). At this point, it is almost as if the universe were testing to see whether you really understand what having abundance is like. Then, the universe (God, higher self, or whichever your belief system has you call upon) assists you in determining whether you feel you deserve an upgrade. And notice how I say *you* feel you deserve an upgrade, versus the universe deciding that for you. You have the power to create as little or as much as you believe you deserve. How much you believe you deserve determines how much is created. How much you believe you deserve is what expedites your "order." Now, visualize this.

Growth is Everywhere

Choose to focus on a vast and open land. It is dawn. Take a walk over this land, barefoot. Notice the moisture and wealth of the soil. Take a moment to feel and smell it. It is very fertile soil. Carefully designate each corner of this land to plant a tree of your liking. Each corner and each tree will represent a different aspect of your life, that which you want to prosper in. One corner can be your money corner. Another corner can be for love and another for health. Once you have decided, find the seeds for each tree. They have been offered to you by a beautiful bird who flies by and lands on the palm of your hand.

Carefully plant the seeds in each corner, simultaneously gifting this land with your beautiful intentions. It is a win-win situation. You offer your gifts to the land, and the land returns these gifts as it cultivates and provides fruit, shade, and beauty.

You notice the sun beginning to rise. The sunrays penetrate each corner of the land and provide the energy the seeds need to grow. Stand back and contemplate the view. As the days pass by, continue to enjoy the magic of nature. Each day you go out to the field and celebrate the growth. Every day counts. Every drop of water you nurture the land with counts. You are as rich as this land. How lucky you are to have so much abundance! How lucky you are to have nature give back to you in such an easy and elegant way!

You deserve to enjoy each fruit you grow. These fruits are the product of your efforts, your dedication, and your faith. Thank nature, and thank yourself. Enjoy your abundance, and continue cultivating. There is more than enough for everyone.

8. CREATING HEALTHY ENERGY FIELDS

Balance and Protection

We are beings of energy. Hence, we connect with everything alive, which includes animals and nature. For the same reason, we are also affected (positively or negatively) by everything alive that we come in contact with. In this case, to be fully balanced, we must not only set the proper intention, we also need to do the work by continually being aware of how we feel and what we sense around other energy beings and energy sources. There are seven main energy centers that govern our bodily fields. (See illustration below.)

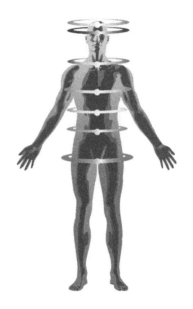

These energy centers, also known as chakras, move in a circular motion. When they are stagnant or cluttered, they will affect us negatively. Therefore, it is very important to clear our energy centers as often as possible. In addition to clearing our energy centers, we also need to create a shield that can serve as protection and preservation of the balance we achieve.

The reason our energy centers become negatively affected is because, if we are not shielded, there is an energy exchange with every live being we come in contact with. Sometimes that energy exchange is of love and gratitude, or at other times, it may be of sadness or anger, to give an example. Allow me to explain further. In addition to our circular energy centers, or chakras, our energy fields expand six feet outward from our bodies in all directions. (See photo below.)

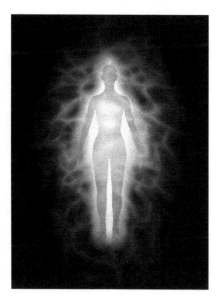

This is why, when you are in line at the grocery store, for instance, and you happen to be close to someone who is very angry and is making mean remarks, you may begin to feel angry and irritable as well. You may think, "That is contagious. Now *I'm* angry too." You are not too far from the truth, especially if your field was wide open. There was an energy exchange, due to your proximity and the fact that you were not shielded at the time.

With our loved ones or acquaintances, the exchange of energy may be even more common, because we have feelings for those people or set opinions about those people that automatically tangle our emotions with theirs. Those of us who are the caregivers of the world may experience this the most. The caregivers of the world, if not shielded, may not be able to identify which energetic charges start with them and which originate from someone else. However, the impact of the energy exchange is a reality for everyone—of any age, culture, or gender.

In Donna Eden's book called *Energy Medicine*, she talks about the importance of energetically balancing yourself. One of her exercises for balancing is called *Heaven Rushing In.* Another is called *Connecting Heaven and Earth.* Along these lines, I will give you a few visuals of my own to achieve balance and to create your protective shield. Bear in mind that you can create your own visuals at any time. Don't let anything stop you. Allow your creativity to flow in order to cater your visualization to your exclusive needs.

Heaven and Earth

> Imagine that you are standing firmly on the ground and that you are barefoot. With your three-dimensional vision, get a sense of what is under your feet—say, six feet under. There are strong, deep roots of a tree planted right below you. Connect with their energy, and imagine that the energy of those roots is moving up towards your feet. Once the energy touches the surface of your feet, allow it to enter your body and watch it move upwards until it reaches

your navel. Once it's there, watch it move in a circular, clockwise motion. Now transfer your focus to above your head. Connect with the sun itself. Watch as its rays travel down until they touch the surface of your head. Welcome them in, and watch as the warm and loving rays travel from your head inward until they, too, reach your navel. Now that both energies (roots of the tree and sun's rays) have met and connected, imagine that the circular clockwise movement of energy is getting larger and growing until you are able to see it covering your entire physical body. (If you can imagine standing with your arms extended out to the sides, the energy should be covering your biofield altogether). See the aura illustration in this Section.

Now, choose your favorite color from oil paints (except black or gray), and trace the external part of the circle that covers you, starting at your feet and going around yourself until it completes the circle at your feet again. This is your shield. You are now grounded, balanced, and protected.

Do this visualization as often as you need to throughout your day. Once you memorize the sequence, you will be able to do so within a few seconds. Remember that balancing and creating a protective shield is not only good for you but also good for others who come in contact with you, so that you do not "spill" or transmit any unbalanced energy. I use this visual right before a patient comes into my office and right after they leave. I open and close my eyes, and I am instantly there. They do not even notice.

Variations and Modifications when Experiencing Difficulties with the Heaven and Earth Visualization

There may be times when this visual is not as easy to follow, so I will give you some variations.

First of all, depending on your preference, you can choose different energy sources to create balance. If you are more of an ocean person, you can replace roots of the tree with the energy of the ocean instead. If you are more of a night person, you can replace the energy of the sun with that of the moon or the stars.

If you are experiencing some difficulty visualizing the energy moving all the way up or down to your navel, focus on the part that is easier. Allow me to further explain:

Perhaps you are working with the roots of the tree, inviting the energy to come into you, and you notice that you cannot see and/or feel the energy move past your knees. Instead of becoming frustrated or uneasy, let it be. Then focus your attention above you, and once the energy of the sun (or moon or stars) touches the surface of your head, welcome it. Allow it to travel through you, past your navel, all the way down to your feet, and then deeper, until it reaches the roots of the tree (or the energy of the ocean, if that is the source you have chosen). Feel the energy from above aiding the energy from below as it pulls it, and then feel both energies travel up to the navel. If the opposite is the case (the energy that is stuck is from above, and you cannot see and/or feel it past your neck), then have the energy from below travel past your navel and go right out to the sun, moon, or stars, to aid it coming down.

Another issue that may be present is the feeling that you cannot anchor yourself well enough. This happens to me every time I come back from a gathering of highly evolved spiritual beings, since we are so far "out of this world" as we work outside of our physical bodies. Therefore, I try to see the roots of the tree deeply planted, but instead I see them floating in the air. So I then envision the roots of the tree large enough to wrap themselves all around the earth and then tie a knot right below the earth. This visual has never failed me, and it really brings me "back to earth."

Becoming the Source

Just for fun, there are times when I feel like becoming the roots of the tree and growing into a full and healthy tree. So I allow the actual roots of the tree to come up, and then I see my body become this magnificent, elegant, and strong tree. My legs are the trunk; my arms and head are the branches. Then, when I connect with the sun, its rays get transferred to every tip of each branch. That's when I see little golden lights coming from the branches; it's as if the fruit of the tree of me is light itself. Then, as a shield, I envision rain coming down and forming a circle around me. This allows me to grow more stable and to continue providing light for the benefit of others, without depleting my energy source.

9. LOVE

Self-Love

Ahhh, how we love to feel loved—yet, how easily we forget to love ourselves! It is my experience as a psychotherapist and healer that, even in the case of the most enlightened and evolved, the search for feeling love becomes external—through others or through something material or achievable: "I need a hug," I will hear, or "I need a lover." People will say, "When I get that new car, I will feel good"; "If I get that new outfit, I am taken care of"; or "When I get promoted, I will feel better about myself." I am not saying that any of those requests or desires are unreasonable. External needs are very valid and necessary. What I am referring to is our sole dependency on them.

Time and time again we hear that love is within us. Of course, we need to believe this and understand it before we can go on a quest to find it within. This quest is no different than the one we embark upon while searching for love from another soul—except the traveling and exploring involves looking at ourselves. How do we do this? For starters, through meditation. If that seems too scary, as it involves being with your own thoughts and discovering yourself, start with visualization.

Follow this next visualization I present to you, and make this one visualization your everyday priority.

Envision walking barefoot through a colorful and aromatic garden. You can delight yourself by admiring your favorite flowers, fully bloomed, and inhaling the fresh, sweet aroma they produce. At the end of the aisle of flowers you are on, you will find a giant pool full of flower petals, all brilliant and naturally scented. This pool is for you. You enter it and enjoy how your body feels against these soft and beautiful petals. Take the time to bring up what your overcritical self considers as your imperfections, including the character traits and history of your choices in life. Use each petal to soften your self-critic and bring to light your beauty. Forgive yourself, and bask in the joy that you are, the love that you are, and what you bring to others and the world. Now slightly open your mouth, as if you were about to sing, and notice flower petals of very unique colors coming out of your mouth. The pool you are in begins to transform itself with your uniqueness. More and more petals come out of you effortlessly, and you finally begin to notice your internal self-love showing its presence externally. Take a close look. Note "That is what my internal self-love looks like. I had it in me all along." Wrap your body around all the petals you created, and promise yourself to always remember to find and love yourself first. Then you can share your love with others and with the world. You are beautiful. You are pure love.

Spreading the Love to Humanity

Awakening Humanity's Heart

Stay centered in your heart. Slowly breathe in and out, until you are able to distinctively sense your heartbeats. Ask your higher self to solely connect with your true essence—pure love. Fill your heart with love by each deep inhalation and exhalation, and feel its power taking over every cell of your body and then growing beyond your physical self.

Find yourself standing right in the middle of the earth. Ground yourself. Notice a large bell by your feet, and begin to ring it. Set the intention within your heart to awaken every human being's heart to the power of their own love. Get a sense that you are watching yourself from above as you ring this bell. Notice how the earth gets brighter and brighter, like little stars sparkling, and looking even closer, see the red hearts beating from everyone joining in this magnificent circle of love. The louder you ring the bell, the more hearts join and open and awaken to love. Breathe deeply, and watch yourself pulling in the rest of the planets and energy systems from above, as the earth and all the heart stars and *you* become one with love. One universe, one species, one heart!

Give thanks to your higher self and to all the universal love. Everything is possible when pure love is at the forefront.

Give yourself a hug, and bring yourself back with your breath. What a powerful being you are! Live life with your heart, and be in love every moment of your existence. Blessings.

10. SPIRITUALITY

Connecting with Your Beliefs: The Divine

Since the beginning of this century, there seems to have been a movement about awakening and connecting to our spiritual selves. People have become fascinated by angels, by meditation, by the natural. I feel that the God force is attempting to bring us back to basics. We are spirit at the core. Our answers are found within. In order to reach within, we cannot avoid the connection with our spiritual selves.

Our beliefs do not have to match. While one person may connect by going to church and following an organized religion, another may find his connection through meditation. As I have said on many occasions throughout this book, what matters is your intention. In this case, your intention is to awaken and connect with your spiritual self. Here is a visualization piece to help you achieve this goal.

The Temple of Connection and Awakening

Find the sunlight, and follow the sunrays with your eyes. Focus on one sunray until you can no longer separate your body from the sunray. You become one. Connect with its warmth, and allow yourself to rise and travel within it. You are now a beam of light in the sky, and you land at the steps of an ancient white temple. Once you land, you enter this temple, leaving the sunray at the doorsteps.

As you walk through the inside of this temple, you see hundreds of beings kneeling in prayer—all dressed in white. Continue walking towards the front altar, until you, also, reach it and kneel in front of it. With your eyes closed, begin to connect with the warmth and love of this space. The sounds of other beings praying or repeating a mantra offer you comfort and peace. You begin to call upon all the divine entities you have faith in, and one by one, they start making their presence known at this altar. Your guardian angel hugs you and spreads his/her wings completely around you, covering you and protecting you with love.

The presence of the Almighty is right in front of you. He kneels at your level and holds your hands, and then He places your hands over His heart. You are overwhelmed by this spiritual awakening and embrace this beautiful moment with all that you are. Take a picture with all your senses, so that this memory remains within forever. Humbly give thanks. Now watch as the Almighty begins to rise above this temple, and as if every being in that temple has light cords, notice how they all connect to the bright light that the Almighty truly is. Your guardian angel does the same. You, too, discover your own light cord and also connect to the Almighty. The light becomes brighter and larger, until you are no longer able to see where it begins and where it ends. This light is everywhere for you to see and connect with. It is a choice.

Find yourself walking back towards the entrance of the temple, and notice how the sunray that brought you there is also interlaced with the heavenly light. It is so bright that you are able to find your own way back home. Once you arrive, you connect with the ground. You are now awakened to your space, but you are also awakened spiritually.

Evolving

Once we awaken to the power of spiritual realism, we will be in constant search for higher plains. There is potential for growth in all that we do. In my opinion, evolving our spiritual selves can be one of the most rewarding experiences a human being can strive for.

I intend to help you with your spiritual growth, as well, by sharing one of my favorite visuals. Open yourselves completely.

Dimensions

Imagine you are standing right in the middle of your backyard or your favorite park. Sense the connection of your physical self with everything alive. Breathe through the leaves of the surrounding trees. Feel the moisture and strength the roots of trees experience. Become one with all that exists. Find yourself expanding sideways and upwards. Your physical self is growing at an accelerated rate. You now perceive your body as being larger than the earth itself. Once you reach higher altitudes, you begin to realize that the limits you knew to be true no longer exist. Instead, with a simple touch, you can cross through to a different dimension. Now you are beyond the galaxies.

You have defied gravity. The dimension you perceive has new colors and new fragrances. Although it is so different from what you know, it feels safe and comforting. You can design your own view and be assured that no other being will have the same view. Later, you find yourself reaching yet another dimension. In this dimension, there is no sense of proportion. With one glance, things may appear large and small simultaneously. Again, design your own view, and be assured nobody else's view will match yours. Continue your growth through more and more dimensions; each represents a new breakthrough. All of these dimensions are completely new to you. There are no limits. You will always be able to reach higher plains. This is you breaking free from your current reality. Dare to expand. Dare to grow. Design your path. You have a say in everything.

Taking your time, begin descending until you reach earth and you recognize the size and shape of your physical self. Slowly begin to move your fingers and your toes. Inhale and exhale as you become aware of your surroundings. Come travel through new dimensions anytime. Your spiritual evolution is endless.

11. Children's Corner

To Encourage Sleeping Alone

Our children are forever on our minds. We worry about them when they are not with us, and we feel like we need a break from them when they are with us. As parents, we are who they look up to. We are who they learn the most from. That includes what we indirectly teach them with the behavior we exhibit around them. Most importantly, because we are the closest to them, they will also absorb many of our energetic vibrations. By this I mean that, how we are feeling when we are around them (even when we think we are hiding it from them) is energetically felt and absorbed by them. Therefore, when we have difficulty separating from them, for instance, it may manifest in them playing that out for us by clinging onto us and having separation-anxiety issues. They may also have trouble sleeping because they may be worried for us and not be conscious about it.

I am not saying that this is the case with every child or that every time a child has trouble sleeping it is because he or she is worried about us. What I am saying is that this aspect of energy exchange needs to be looked at and considered before we make them fully responsible for an issue.

On the other hand, given children's purity and vast imagination, it may be much easier for them to overcome some of the issues pointed above. Children are great at visualization. Furthermore, since you (the parent) will most likely be the person delivering the visualization piece, it's likely that you, too, will clear whatever aspects of the issue you are helping them resolve.

Following is a visualization piece that will help them sleep alone in their own rooms.

Sweet Dreams

While tucking your child into bed, have her close her eyes and follow you on an imaginary journey. Start by asking her to breathe in and out as if she were first filling up a balloon with air as she inhales and then letting the air out of the balloon as she exhales. (Use this breathing visual to help her relax anytime she is anxious). Then follow this script:

> You are flying above the trees, on your way to a magical and very sweet land. The sun is shining brightly. You slowly fly downward until your feet touch the ground.
>
> The moment you land, you can smell all kinds of sweet treats. As you look around, you notice that there is a long river that is as white as cotton. You go to touch it and realize it is milk. Yum! You would give anything to have some chocolate chip cookies to enjoy with this milk. And when you look up, you notice that the

trees around you grow chocolate chip cookies. You run to get some and dip each cookie into the river of milk. That is so-o-o delicious! You also wish you had some marshmallows. And, what do you know? The small flowers are actually marshmallows! So you begin to realize that whatever you wish for becomes true in this land.

Here comes a lovely wizard to give you all the rules of this land. He says, "All your food wishes can come true in this land, but it only works when you are sleeping in your own bed. Once you enter the magical land of sweets, you will always be protected from bad dreams and from any scary thoughts. All is safe, beautiful, and tasty in this land. Come visit every night, and you can even bring your favorite stuffed animal with you to have fun."

"This is perfect," you say. "I love it here!" And you can stay there and safely fall asleep and return when it is time to wake up. We love you, sweetheart! Sweet dreams.

To Reduce Separation Anxiety

Separation anxiety occurs mainly because the child experiences a fear that he may not see you (parent) again, or he may not feel safe enough without you by his side. This is a very common feeling for younger children. Yet, separation anxiety can also be developed after a traumatic event in which the parent was unable to be present at a time when expected.

Following are a few ideas to physically help children with separation anxiety.

Every child has a transitional object. This object can be anything from a stuffed animal, to a doll, to a blanket, to a picture. What is important is that he feels safe because he has something familiar in hand. The sense of safety can be enhanced by a familiar smell. If you provide your child with a piece of your clothing and use your perfume on it, he may automatically feel your presence even if you are not physically with him. Try this if you are dropping him off at a nanny's house, or place the clothing inside his backpack before he goes to school. Let him know that, to avoid embarrassment, he can go to the restroom with his backpack to hold the garment for reassurance.

Another idea is to record a sweet voice mail that he can replay if he is spending the night with someone else.

Finally, help him with the following visual, which you may also choose to record for him.

I Am Always with You

> Stand tall, right in the middle of your favorite room. Imagine that I am hugging you and letting you know how much you are loved. Keep a mental picture of our hug, and now wrap us in a giant bubble. Remember, you are inside this bubble with me. Wherever you go, you will travel inside this bubble. Nobody else can see

me. People can only see you. You are so clever to fool them, because I am with you wherever you go. You are safe, and you can relax now.

Concentration and Homework

For many parents, the battles they endure with their children when trying to have them concentrate on their homework can be quite frustrating. The fact remains that most children (and adults, for that matter) have an easier time concentrating on what they enjoy. This is the reason why even children diagnosed with attention deficit disorder are able to play video games for hours without blinking or losing interest. They are enjoying what they are engaged in. Therefore, as a parent, you need to find the magical formula to make your children's homework interesting. This will be different from child to child, as their interests are varied. However, you, the parent, know your child better than anyone. Therefore, find the themes that interest your child the most, and start using them with homework. This can be as simple as incorporating a vocabulary associated with their favorite theme or interests. For instance, if your child loves football, explain things using terms like *tackle*, *a few yards to go*, *touchdown*, etc. Another example is to not limit the lesson to a chair and desk. If you need to go outside with them, do so. Also, be aware how long your child's attention span is before she starts to wander. If it is fifteen minutes, then break the lesson into fifteen-minute increments. Give her five-minute breaks in between, encouraging her to stretch or have a snack. Set the alarm, and back you go to the lesson, until it is completed.

Another example that may surprise you is the use of music to concentrate. During their psychotherapy visits with me, many teens have confided that they are better able to concentrate while they are listening to music. Test your child. If she studies with music and she is getting better grades, allow her to do so.

As well, help your child determine whether it is easier for him to learn by reading and then having a vivid picture in his head about the pages he is reading, or whether he prefers imagining a scene playing out in his head about what he is trying to learn. Remind him of this tool, especially when he needs to memorize a lot of facts. If, however, your child states that he learns better by what he hears, then have him record his own voice while reading his study materials out loud.

Finally, you can guide your child through the relaxation visual found in Part I, Section 2 prior to him beginning his homework. This should help you both with patience and focus.

PART III

Transcending the Vision

1. WHAT'S NEXT?

Now that you have experienced visualization on a very personal level, you are ready to transcend the vision. Simply stated, you can now also utilize visualization to help the rest of the world! You may choose to envision a harmonious administration for the company you work for. You can visualize optimum health for family members who are ill. You may want to daydream about a world that is war free and hunger free. You may also choose to start a visualization group and utilize this book as your guide. From the smallest to the largest of groups, through visualization, you have the power to positively influence anything. The possibilities are endless, because our imaginations have no limits. Create any theme and, in a meditative state, awaken your creative self. Daydream! Allow yourself to expand your vision. Each time push yourself further. Find your *self* within, and dare to take charge of the outcome of your life as well as that of the world. All you need to do is *visualize*.

2. VISUALIZE YOURSELF: THE PROMISE

The light is shining right above me. The light is now within me. I now can see it all so very clearly. I visualize myself in love, in harmony with life and with others, in perfect health, energized, and whole.

I am now aware. I have now awakened to endless possibilities and to my own creative power. I choose to remain awake. I promise myself that I will remain awake while actively participating in my life's endeavors. I am a visualizer.

ABOUT THE AUTHOR

Aileen Nealie has been a licensed psychotherapist in the state of California since 2003. On her quest to deliver a more holistic treatment to her patients in private practice and through her workshops, in 2008 she became a Diplomate in Comprehensive Energy Psychology and was proud to belong to the first group ever to accomplish this title through ACEP (Association for Comprehensive Energy Psychology). From 2010 to 2011 Ms. Nealie inspired thousands through her own radio talk show with World Talk Radio. Her show *Holistic Answers to Mental Health* quickly became the 4th most listened program on World Talk Radio.

Ms. Nealie is a well respected speaker (both in English and Spanish) and workshop facilitator in the area of Energy Psychology. She is the creator of several visualization CDs including: *Over Sea Over Sky* (a peaceful and creative relaxation

CD); *Encontrando Mi Voz* Finding My Voice (an empowerment CD in Spanish); *The Sacred OR* (healing layers of pain with divine entities and higher self in the operating room); and *Chakra Balancing with Nature*. These can be purchased through her website at: www.AileenNealieTherapies.com.

In 2011 her creative visualization techniques inspired her to establish **The Center for Tranquility and Restoration**, a place she calls "The Gym for the Soul," where individuals can experience themed guided visualizations by the hour in a group setting facilitated by Ms. Nealie. Her center and practice are based in Los Angeles, CA. She also works with patients over the phone or through Skype.

Ms. Nealie comes from a lineage of spiritual healers. She is committed to reaching as many people as possible—to help them experience her visualization gifts and help them establish a daily practice of visualization, while designing the outcomes of their lives, one issue at a time.

CPSIA information can be obtained
at www.ICGtesting.com
Printed in the USA
FSHW012001071118
53637FS